On the Good of Widowhood

On the Good of Widowhood

St. Augustine

On the Good of Widowhood
© Lighthouse Publishing 2018

Written by: St. Augustine (Nov.13 354 – Aug.28 430)

Translated by: Rev. C. L. Cornish. M.A.

Updated into Modern U.S English by A.M. Overett (b. 1960)

All rights reserved. Without limiting the rights under copyright reserved above, no part of this publication may be reproduced, stored in a retrieval system, or transmitted, in any form or by any means (electronic, mechanical, photocopying, recording or otherwise), without the prior written permission of the copyright owner of this book.

Published by
Lighthouse Christian Publishing
SAN 257-4330
5531 Dufferin Drive
Savage, Minnesota, 55378
United States of America

www.lighthousechristianpublishing.com

Introductory Notice.

This work is not mentioned in the Retractations, probably because it is a letter, and as such it is reckoned by Possidius, cap. 7. It is also marked as St. Augustin's by its references to his other works, De Bono Conjugali, etc. cap. 15. Ep. to Proba, cap. 23. The date is marked by the recent consecration of Demetrias, which was in 413. The admonition for which he is thanked by Juliana, Ep. 188, may be that against Pelagianism. An objection has been raised from its disagreement with the fourth Council of Carthage, an. 398. can. 104, which excommunicates widows who marry again after consecration, and pronounces them guilty of adultery, whereas in cap. 10 and 11, the opinion that such marriages are no marriages, and that they ought to return to continence, is refuted. The two, however, are not wholly irreconcilable, as there may be a guilt similar to that of adultery incurred, and it may be visited with a censure in the form of excommunication, and yet the marriage may remain valid. The 16th Canon of Chalcedon imposes such a penalty, with power to the Bishop to relax it. —Abridged from the Benedictine Edition.

Augustin the Bishop, servant of Christ, and of the servants of Christ, unto the religious handmaiden of God, Juliana, in the Lord of lords health. Not any longer to be in debt of my promise to your request and love in Christ, I have seized the occasion as I could, amid other my very pressing engagements, to write to you somewhat concerning the profession of holy widowhood, forasmuch as, when I was present, you laded me with entreaty, and, when I had not been able to deny you this, you often by letters demanded my promise. And in this work of ours, when you shall find in reading that some things pertain not at all unto your own person, or unto the person of you, who are living together in Christ, nor are strictly necessary to give counsel unto your life, it will be your duty not on this account to judge them superfluous. Forsooth this letter, although it be addressed to you, was not to be written for you alone; but certainly it was a matter for us not to neglect, that it should profit others also through your means. Whatsoever, therefore, you shall find here, such as either hath been at no time necessary for you, or is not so now, and which yet you shall perceive to be necessary for others, grieve not either to possess or to lend to read; that your charity also may be the profit of others.

2. Whereas, therefore, in every question, which relates to life and conduct, not only teaching, but exhortation also is necessary; in order that by teaching we may know what is to be done, and by exhortation may be incited not to think it irksome to do what we already know is to be done; what more can I teach you, than what we read in the Apostle? For holy Scripture set a rule to our teaching, that we dare not "be wise more than it

behooves to be wise;" but be wise, as himself saith, "unto soberness, according as unto each God hath allotted the measure of faith." Be it not therefore for me to teach you any other thing, save to expound to you the words of the Teacher, and to treat of them as the Lord shall have given to me.

3. Therefore (thus) saith the Apostle, the teacher of the Gentiles, the vessel of election, "But I say unto the unmarried and the widows, that it is good for them, if they shall have so continued, even as I also." These words are to be so understood, as that we think not that widows ought not to be called unmarried, in that they seem to have made trial of marriage: for by the name of unmarried women he means those, who are not now bound by marriage, whether they have been, or whether they have not been so. And this in another place he opens, where he says, "Divided is a woman unmarried and a virgin." Assuredly when he adds a virgin also, what would he have understood by an unmarried woman, but a widow? Whence also, in what follows, under the one term "unmarried" he embraces both professions, saying, "She who is unmarried is careful of the things of the Lord, how to please the Lord: but she who is married is careful of the things of the world, how to please her husband." Certainly, by the unmarried he would have understood, not only her who hath never married, but her also, who, being by widowhood set free from the bond of marriage, hath ceased to be married; for on this account also he called not married, save her, who hath a husband; not her also, who hath had, and hath not. Wherefore every widow is unmarried; but, because not every unmarried woman is a widow, for there are virgins also; therefore he hath here

set both, where he says, "But I say unto the unmarried and the widows;" as if he should say, What I say unto the unmarried, I say not unto them alone, who are virgins, but unto them also who are widows; "that it is good for them, if they shall have so continued, even as also I."

4. Lo, there is your good compared to that good, which the Apostle calls his own, if faith be present: yea, rather, because faith is present. Short is this teaching, yet not on this account to be despised, because it is short; but on this account to be retained the more easily and the more dearly, in that in shortness it is not cheap. For it is not every kind of good so ever, which the Apostle would here set forth, which he hath unambiguously placed above the faith of married women. But how great good the faith of married women, that is, of Christian and religious women joined in marriage, hath, may be understood from this, that, when he was giving charge for the avoiding of fornication, wherein assuredly he was addressing married persons also, he saith, "Know ye not that your bodies are the members of Christ?" So great then is the good of faithful marriage, that even the very members are (members) of Christ. But, forasmuch as the good of widowed continence is better than this good, the purpose of this profession is, not that a catholic widow be anything more than a member of Christ, but that she have a better place, than a married woman, among the members of Christ. Forsooth the same Apostle says, "For, as in one body we have many members, but all members have not the same course of action; so being many we are one body in Christ, and each members one of another: having gifts diverse according unto the grace, which hath been given unto us."

5. Wherefore also when he was advising married persons not to defraud one another of the due of carnal intercourse; lest, by this means, the one of them, (the due of marriage being denied to him,) being through his own incontinence tempted of Satan, should fall away into fornication, he saith, "But this I say of leave, not of command; but I would that all men were as I myself; but each one hath his own proper gift from God; but one in this way, and another in that." You see that wedded chastity also, and the marriage faith of the Christian bed, is a "gift," and this of God; so that, when as carnal lust exceeds somewhat the measure of sensual intercourse, beyond what is necessary for the begetting of children, this evil is not of marriage, but venial by reason of the good of marriage. For not concerning marriage, which is contracted for the begetting of children, and the faith of wedded chastity, and the sacrament (indissoluble, so long as both live) of matrimony, all which are good; but concerning that immoderate use of the flesh, which is recognized in the weakness of married persons, and is pardoned by the intervention of the good of marriage, the Apostle saith, "I speak of leave, not of command." Also, when he says, "The woman is bound, so long as her husband lives: but, in case her husband shall have died, she is set free: let her be married to whom she will, only in the Lord: but she shall be more blessed, if she shall have so continued, according to my counsel;" he shows sufficiently that a faithful woman is blessed in the Lord, even when she marries a second time after the death of her husband, but that a widow is more blessed in the same Lord; that is, to speak not only in the words, but by instances also, of the Scriptures, that Ruth is blessed, but that Anna is more blessed.

6. Wherefore this in the first place you ought to know, that by the good, which you have chosen, second marriages are not condemned, but are set in lower honor. For, even as the good of holy virginity, which thy daughter hath chosen, doth not condemn thy one marriage; so neither doth thy widowhood the second marriage of any. For hence, specially, the heresies of the Cataphryges and of the Novatians swelled, which Tertullian also, inflated with cheeks full of sound not of wisdom, whilst with railing tooth he attacks second marriages, as though unlawful, which the Apostle with sober mind allows to be altogether lawful. From this soundness of doctrine let no man's reasoning, be he unlearned, or be he learned, move thee; nor do thou so extol thy own good, as to charge as evil that of another's which is not evil; but do thou rejoice so much the more of thy own good, the more thou sees, that, by it, not only are evils shunned, but some goods too surpassed. For adultery and fornication are evils. But from these unlawful things she is very far removed, who hath bound herself by liberty of vow, and, not by command of law, but by counsel of charity, hath brought to pass that even things lawful should not be lawful to her. And marriage chastity is a good, but widowed continence is a better good. Therefore, this better good is honored by the submission of that other, not that other condemned by the praise of this that is better.

7. But whereas the Apostle, when commending the fruit of unmarried men and women, in that they have thought of the things of the Lord, how to please God, added and saith, "But this I say for your profit, not to cast a snare on you," that is, not to force you; "but in order to

that which is honorable;" we ought not, because he saith that the good of the unmarried is honorable, therefore to think that the bond of marriage is base; otherwise we shall condemn first marriages also, which neither Cataphryges, nor Novatians, nor their most learned upholder Tertullian dared to call base. But as, when he says, "But I say unto the unmarried and widows, that it is good for them if they shall have so continued;" assuredly he set down "good" for "better," since everything, which, when compared with a good, is called better, this also without doubt is a good; for what else is it that it is so called better, save that it is more good? and yet we do not on this account suppose him by consequence to have thought that it was an evil, in case they married, in that he said, "it is good for them, if they shall have so continued;" so also, when he says, "but in order to that which is honest," he hath not shown that marriage is base, but that which was more honest than (another thing also) honest, he hath commended by the name of honest in general. Because what is more honest, save what is more honest? But what is more honest is certainly honest. Forsooth he plainly showed that this is better than that other that is good, where he says, "Whoso giveth to marry, doeth well; but whoso giveth not to marry, doeth better." And this more blessed than that other that is blessed, where he saith, "But she shall be more blessed, if she shall have so continued." As, therefore, there is than good a better, and than blessed a more blessed, so is there than honest a more honest, which he chose to call honest. For far be it that that be base, of which the Apostle Peter speaking saith, "Husbands, unto your wives, as unto the weaker and subject vessel, give honor, as unto co-heirs of grace;" and addressing the wives, he exhorts them, by the pattern of

Sarah, to be subject unto their husbands; "For so," saith he, "certain holy women, who hoped in God, adorned themselves, obeying their own husbands; even as Sarah obeyed Abraham, calling him lord, whose daughters ye are made, well-doing, and not fearing any disturbance."

8. Whence, also, what the Apostle Paul said of the unmarried woman, "that she may be holy both in body and spirit;" we are not so to understand, as though a faithful woman being married and chaste, and according to the Scriptures subject unto her husband, be not holy in body, but only in spirit. For it cannot come to pass, that when the spirit is sanctified, the body also be not holy, of which the sanctified spirit makes use: but, that we seem not to any to argue rather than to prove this by divine saying; since the Apostle Peter, making mention of Sarah, saith only "holy women," and saith not, "and in body;" let us consider that saying of the same Paul, where forbidding fornication he saith, "Know ye not, that your bodies are members of Christ? Taking, therefore, members of Christ, shall I make them members of a harlot? Far be it." Therefore, let anyone dare to say that the members of Christ are not holy; or let him not dare to separate from the members of Christ the bodies of the faithful that are married. Whence, also, a little after he saith, "Your body is the temple within you of the Holy Spirit, Whom ye have from God; and ye are not your own; for ye have been bought with a great price." He saith that the body of the faithful is both members of Christ, and the temple of the Holy Spirit, wherein assuredly the faithful of both sexes are understood. There therefore are married women, there unmarried women also; but distinct in their deserts, and as members preferred to members,

whilst yet neither are separated from the body. Whereas, therefore, he saith, speaking of an unmarried woman, "that she may be holy both in body and spirit," he would have understood a fuller sanctification both in body and in spirit, and hath not deprived the body of married women of all sanctification.

9. Learn, therefore, that thy good, yea, rather, remember what thou hast learned, that thy good is more praised, because there is another good than which this is better, than if this could not on any other condition be a good, unless that were an evil, or altogether were not. The eyes have great honor in the body, but they would have less, if they were alone, and there were not other members of less honor. In heaven itself the sun by its light surpasses, not chides, the moon; and star from star differs in glory, not is at variance through pride. Therefore, "God made all things, and, lo, very good;" not only "good," but also "very;" for no other reason, than because "all." For of each several work throughout it was also said, "God saw that it is good." But, when "all" were named, "very" was added; and it was said, "God saw all things which He made, and, lo, very good." For certain several things were better than other several, but all together better than any several. Therefore, may the sound doctrine of Christ make thee in His Body sound through His Grace, that, what thou hast better than others in body and spirit, the self-same thy spirit, which ruled the body, may neither extol with insolence, nor distinguish with lack of knowledge.

10. Nor, because I called Ruth blessed, Anna more blessed, in that the former married twice, the latter, being soon widowed of her one husband, so lived long, do you

straightway also think that you are better than Ruth. Forsooth different in the times of the Prophets was the dispensation of holy females, whom obedience, not lust, forced to marry, for the propagation of the people of God, that in them Prophets of Christ might be sent beforehand; whereas the People itself also, by those things which in figure happened among them, whether in the case of those who knew, or in the case of those who knew not those things, was nothing else than a Prophet of Christ, of whom should be born the Flesh also of Christ. In order therefore for the propagation of that people, he was accounted accursed by sentence of the Law, whoso raised not up seed in Israel. Whence also holy women were kindled, not by lust of sensual intercourse, but by piety of bearing; so that we most rightly believe of them that they would not have sought sensual intercourse, in case a family could have come by any other means. And to the husbands was allowed the use of several wives living; and that the cause of this was not lust of the flesh, but forethought of begetting, is shown by the fact, that, as it was lawful for holy men to have several wives living, it was not likewise lawful for holy women to have intercourse with several husbands living; in that they would be by so much the baser, by how much the more they sought what would not add to their fruitfulness. Wherefore holy Ruth, not having seed such as at that time was necessary in Israel, on the death of her husband sought another of whom to have it. Therefore than this one twice married, Anna once married a widow was on this account more blessed, in that she attained also to be a prophetess of Christ; concerning whom we are to believe, that, although she had no sons, (which indeed Scripture by keeping silence hath left uncertain,) yet, had she by that Spirit foreseen that Christ would immediately come of a virgin, by Which she was enabled to recognize Him even as a child: whence, with good reason, even without sons, (that is, assuming she had none,) she refused a second marriage: in that she knew that now was the time wherein Christ were better served, not by duty of bearing, but by zeal of containing: not by fruitfulness of married womb, but by chastity of widowed conduct. But if Ruth also was aware that by her flesh was propagated a seed, whereof Christ should hereafter have flesh, and by marrying set forth her ministering to this knowledge, I dare not any longer say that the widowhood of Anna was more blessed than her fruitfulness.

11. But thou who both hast sons, and lives in that end of the world, wherein now is the time not of casting stones, but of gathering; not of embracing, but of abstaining from embracing; when the Apostle cries out, "But this I say, brethren, the time is short; it remains, that both they who have wives be as not having;" assuredly if thou has sought a second marriage, it would have been no obedience of prophecy or law, no carnal desire even of family, but a mark of incontinence alone. For you would have done what the Apostle says, after he had said, "It is good for them, if they shall have so continued, even as I;" forsooth he straightway added, "But if they contain not themselves, let them marry; for I had rather that they marry than be burned." For this he said, in order that the evil of unbridled desire might not be carried headlong into criminal baseness, being taken up by the honest estate of marriage. But thanks be to the Lord, in that thou hast given birth to what thou would not be, and the virginity of thy child hath compensated for the loss of thy virginity.

For Christian doctrine, having diligent question made of it, makes answer, that a first marriage also now at this time is to be despised, unless incontinence stand in the way. For he, who said, "If they contain not themselves, let them marry," could have said, "If they have not sons, let them marry," if, when now after the Resurrection and Preaching of Christ, there is unto all nations so great and abundant supply of sons to be spiritually begotten, it were any such duty to beget sons after the flesh as it was in the first times. And, whereas in another place he saith, "But I will that the younger marry, bear children, be mothers of families," he commends with apostolic sobriety and authority the good of marriage, but doth not impose the duty of bearing, as though in order to obey the law, even on those who "receive" the good of continence. Lastly, why he had said this, he unfolds, when he adds and says, "To give no occasion of speaking evil to the adversary; for already certain have turned back after Satan:" that by these words of his we may understand, that those, whom he would have marry, could have done better to contain than marry; but better to marry than to go back after Satan, that is, to fall away from that excellent purpose of virginal or widowed chastity, by looking back to things that are behind, and perish. Wherefore, such as contain not themselves, let them marry before they make profession of continence, before they vow unto God, what, if they pay not, they are justly condemned. Forsooth in another place he saith of such, "For when they have lived in delights in Christ, they wish to marry: having condemnation, in that they have made of none effect their first faith;" that is, they have turned aside their will from the purpose of continence unto marriage. Forsooth they have made of none effect the faith, whereby they formerly vowed what they were unwilling by perseverance to fulfill. Therefore, the good of marriage is indeed ever a good: but in the people of God it was at one time an act of obedience unto the law; now it is a remedy for weakness, but in certain a solace of human nature. Forsooth to be engaged in the getting of children, not after the fashion of dogs by promiscuous use of females, but by honest order of marriage, is not an affection such as we are to blame in a man; yet this affection itself the Christian mind, having thoughts of heavenly things, in a more praiseworthy manner surpasses and overcomes.

12. But since, as the Lord saith, "Not all receive this word;" therefore let her who can receive it, receive it; and let her, who contained not, marry; let her, who hath not begun, deliberate; let her, who hath undertaken it, persevere; let there be no occasion given unto the adversary, let there be no oblation withdrawn from Christ. Forsooth in the marriage bond if chastity be preserved, condemnation is not feared; but in widowed and virginal continence, the excellence of a greater gift is sought for: and, when this has been sought, and chosen, and by debt of vow offered, from this time not only to enter upon marriage, but, although one be not married, to wish to marry is matter of condemnation. For, in order to show this, the Apostle saith not, "When they shall have lived in delights, in Christ" they marry; but "they wish to marry; having," saith he, "condemnation, in that they have made of none effect their first faith," although not by marrying, yet by wishing; not that the marriages even of such are judged matter of condemnation; but there is condemned a wrong done to purpose, there is condemned a broken faith of vow, there is condemned not a relief by lower good,

but a fall from higher good: lastly, such are condemned, not because they have entered upon marriage faith afterwards, but because they have made of none effect the first faith of continence. And in order to suggest this in few words, the Apostle would not say, that they have condemnation, who after purpose of greater sanctity marry, (not because they are not condemned, but lest in them marriage itself should be thought to be condemned:) but, after he had said, "they wish to marry," he straightway added, "having condemnation." And he stated the reason, "in that they have made of none effect their former faith," in order that it may appear that it is the will which fell away from its purpose, which is condemned, whether marriage follow, or fail to follow.

13. Wherefore they who say that the marriages of such are not marriages, but rather adulteries, seem not to me to consider with sufficient acuteness and care what they say; forsooth they, are misled by a semblance of truth. For, whereas they, who of Christian sanctity marry not, are said to choose the marriage of Christ, hence certain argue saying, If she, who during the life of her husband is married to another, be an adulteress, even as the Lord Himself hath laid down in the Gospel; therefore, during the life of Christ, over Whom death hath no more dominion, if she who had chosen His marriage, be married to a man, she is an adulteress. They, who say this, are moved indeed with acuteness, but fail to observe, how great absurdity in fact follows on this reasoning. For whereas it is praiseworthy that, even during the life of her husband, by his consent, a female vow continence unto Christ, now, according to the reasoning of these persons, no one ought to do this, lest she make Christ Himself,

what is impious to imagine, an adulterer, by being married to Him during the life of her husband. Next, whereas first marriages are of better desert than second, far be it that this be the thought of holy widows, that Christ seem unto them as a second husband. For Himself they used heretofore also to have, (when they were subject and did faithful service to their own husbands,) not after the flesh, but after the Spirit a Husband; unto Whom the Church herself, of which they are members, is the wife; who by soundness of faith, of hope, of charity, not in the virgins alone, but in widows also, and faithful married women, is altogether a virgin. Forsooth unto the universal Church, of which they all are members, the Apostle saith, "I joined you unto one husband a chaste virgin to present unto Christ." But He knows how to make fruitful, without marring of chastity, a wife a virgin, Whom even in the flesh itself His Mother could without violation of chastity conceive. But there is brought to pass by means of this ill-considered notion, (whereby they think that the marriages of women who have fallen away from this holy purpose, in case they shall have married, are no marriages,) no small evil, that wives be separated from their husbands, as though they were adulteresses, not wives; and wishing to restore to continence the women thus separated, they make their husbands real adulterers, in that during the life of their wives they have married others.

14. Wherefore I cannot indeed say, of females who have fallen away from a better purpose, in case they shall have married, that they are adulteries, not marriages; but I plainly would not hesitate to say, that departures and fallings away from a holier chastity, which is vowed unto

the Lord, are worse than adulteries. For if, what may no way be doubted, it pertains unto an offense against Christ, when a member of Him kept not faith to her husband; how much graver offense is it against Him, when unto Himself faith is not kept, in a matter which He requires when offered, Who had not required that it should be offered. For when each fails to render that which, not by force of command, but by advice of counsel, he vowed, by so much the more doth he increase the unrighteousness of the wrong done to his vow, by how much the less necessity he had to vow. These matters I for this reason treat of, that you may not think either that second marriages are criminal, or that any marriages whatsoever, being marriages, are an evil. Therefore let this be your mind, not that you condemn them, but that you despise them. Therefore the good of widowed chastity is becoming after a brighter fashion, in that in order to make vow and profession of it, females may despise what is both pleasing and lawful. But after profession of vow made they must continue to rein in, and overcome, what is pleasing, because it is no longer lawful.

15. Men are wanting to move a question concerning a third or fourth marriage, and even more numerous marriages than this. On which to make answer strictly, I dare neither to condemn any marriage, nor to take from these the shame of their great number. But, lest the brevity of this my answer may chance to displease any, I am prepared to listen to my reprover treating more fully. For perhaps he alleges some reason, why second marriages be not condemned, but third be condemned. For I, as in the beginning of this discourse I gave warning, dare not to be wiser than it behooves to be wise. For who

am I, that I should think that that must be defined which I see that the Apostle hath not defined? For he saith, "A woman is bound, so long as her husband lives." He said not, her first; or, second; or, third; or, fourth; but, "A woman," saith he, "is bound, so long as her husband lives; but if her husband shall be dead, she is set free; let her be married to whom she will, only in the Lord: but she shall be more blessed, if she shall have so continued." I know not what can be added to, or taken from, this sentence, so far as relates to this matter. Next I hear Himself also, the Master and Lord of the Apostles and of us, answering the Sadducees, when they had proposed to Him a woman not once-married, or twice-married, but, if it can be said, seven-married, whose wife she should be in the resurrection? For rebuking them, He saith, "Ye do err, not knowing the Scriptures, nor the power of God. For in the resurrection they shall neither be married, nor marry wives; for they shall not begin to die, but shall be equal to the Angels of God." Therefore He made mention of their resurrection, who shall rise again unto life, not who shall rise again unto punishment. Therefore He might have said, Ye do err, knowing not the Scriptures, nor the power of God: for in that resurrection it will not be possible that there be those that were wives of many; and then added, that neither doth any there marry. But neither, as we see, did He in this sentence show any sign of condemning her who was the wife of so many husbands. Wherefore neither dare I, contrary to the feeling of natural shame, say, that, when her husbands are dead, a woman marry as often as she will; nor dare I, out of my own heart, beside the authority of holy Scripture, condemn any number of marriages whatever. But, what I say to a widow, who hath had one husband, this I say to every widow; you will be more blessed, if you shall have so continued.

16. For that also is no foolish question which is wont to be proposed, that whoso can may say, which widow is to be preferred in desert; whether one who hath had one husband, who, after having lived a considerable time with her husband, being left a widow with sons born to her and alive, hath made profession of continence; or she who as a young woman having lost two husbands within two years, having no children left alive to console her, hath vowed to God continence, and in it hath grown old with most enduring sanctity. Herein let them exercise themselves, if they can, by discussing, and by showing some proof to us, who weigh the merits of widows by number of husbands, not by the strength itself of continence. For, if they shall have said, that she who hath had one husband is to be preferred to her who hath had two; unless they shall have alleged some special reason or authority, they will assuredly be found to set before excellence of soul, not greater excellence of soul, but good fortune of the flesh. Forsooth it pertained unto good fortune of the flesh, both to live a long time with her husband, and to conceive sons. But, if they prefer her not on this account, that she had sons; at any rate the very fact that she lived a long time with her husband, what else was it than good fortune of the flesh? Further, the desert of Anna herself is herein chiefly commended, in that, after she had so soon buried her husband, through her protracted life she long contended with the flesh, and overcame. For so it is written, "And there was Anna, a prophetess, the daughter of Phanuel, of the tribe of Aser; she was far advanced in many days; and had lived with her husband seven years from her virginity; and she was a

Of Holy Virginity

widow even unto eighty-four years, who used not to depart from the Temple, by fastings and prayers serving day and night." You see how the holy widow is not only commended in this, that she had had one husband, but also, that she had lived few years with a husband from her virginity, and had with so great service of piety continued her office of widowed chastity even unto so great age.

17. Let us therefore set before our eyes three widows, each having one of the things, the whole of which were in her: let us suppose one who had had one husband, in whose case is wanting both so great length of widowhood, in that she hath lived long with her husband, and so great zeal of piety, in that she doth not so serve with fasts and prayers: a second, who after the very short life of her former husband, had quickly lost a second also, and is now long time a widow, but yet herself also doth not so set herself to the most religious service of fasts and prayers: a third, who not only hath had two husbands, but also hath lived long with each of them singly, or with one of them, and being left a widow at a later period of life, wherein indeed, in case she had wished to marry, she might also conceive sons, hath taken upon her widowed continence; but is more intent on God, more careful to do always the things that please Him, day and night, like Anna, serving by prayers and fasts. If a question be raised, which of these is to be preferred in deserts, who but must see that in this contest the palm must be given to the greater and, more glowing piety? So also if three others be set, in each of whom are two of those three, but one of the three in each wanting, who can doubt that they will be the better, who shall have in a more excellent manner in their two goods pious humility, in order that

there may be lofty piety?

18. No one indeed of these six widows could come up to your standard. For you, in case that you shall have maintained this vow even unto old age, mayest have all the three things wherein the desert of Anna excelled. For both thou hast had one husband, and he lived not long with thee in the flesh; and, by this means, in case that thou shall show forth obedience to the words of the Apostle, saying, "But she who is a widow indeed and desolate, hath hoped in the Lord, and persevered in prayers night and day," and with sober watchfulness shall shun what follows, "But she who passes her time in delights, living is dead," all those three goods, which were Anna's, shall be thine also. But you have sons also, which haply she had not. And yet you are not on this account to be praised, that you have them, but that you are zealous to nurture and educate them piously. For that they were born to thee, was of fruitfulness; that they are alive, is of good fortune; that they be so brought up, is of your will and disposal. In the former let men congratulate you, in this let them imitate you. Anna, through prophetic knowledge, recognized Christ with His virgin Mother; thee the grace of the Gospel hath made the mother of a virgin of Christ. Therefore that holy virgin, whom herself willing and seeking it ye have offered unto Christ, hath added something of virginal desert also unto the widowed deserts of her grandmother and mother. For ye who have her, fail not to have something thence; and in her ye are, what in yourselves ye are not. For that holy virginity should be taken from you at your marriage, was on this account brought to pass, in order that she should be born of you.

19. These discussions, therefore, concerning the different deserts of married women, and of different widows, I would not in this work enter upon, if, what I am writing unto you, I were writing only for you. But, since there are in this kind of discourse certain very difficult questions, it was my wish to say something more than what properly relates to you, by reason of certain, who seem not to themselves learned, unless they essay, not by passing judgment to discuss, but by rending to cut in pieces the labors of others: in the next place, that you yourself also may not only keep what you have vowed, and make advance in that good; but also know more carefully and more surely, that this same good of yours is not distinguished from the evil of marriage, but is set before the good of marriage. For let not such, as condemn the marriage of widowed females, although they exercise their continence in abstaining from many things, which you make use of, on this account lead you astray, to think what they think, although you cannot do what they do. For no one would be a madman, although he see that the strength of a madman is greater than of men in their sound senses. Chiefly, therefore, let sound doctrine both adorn and guard goodness of purpose. Forsooth it is from this cause that catholic females, even after that they have been married more than once, are by just judgment preferred, not only to the widows who have had one husband, but also to the virgins of heretics. There are indeed on these three matters, of marriage, widowhood, and virginity, many winding recesses of questions, many perplexities; and in order by discussion to enter deeply into and solve these, there is required both greater care, and a fuller discourse; that either we may have a right mind in all those things, or, if in any matter we be

otherwise minded, this also God may reveal unto us. However, what there also the Apostle saith next after, "Whereunto we have arrived, in that let us walk." But we have arrived, in what relates to this matter on which we are speaking, so far as to set continence before marriage, but holy virginity even before widowed continence; and not to condemn any marriages, which yet are not adulteries but marriages, by praise of any purpose whatever of our own or of our friends. Many other things on these matters we have said in a Book concerning the Good of Marriage, and in another Book concerning Holy Virginity, and in a Book which we composed with as great pains as we could against Faustus the Manichee; since, by most biting reproaches in his writings of the chaste marriages of Patriarchs and Prophets, he had turned aside the minds of certain unlearned persons from soundness of faith.

20. Wherefore, forasmuch as in the beginning of this little work I had proposed certain two necessary matters, and had undertaken to follow them out; one which related to doctrine, the other to exhortation; and I have not failed in the former part, to the best of my power, according to the business which I had undertaken; let us come to exhortation, in order that the good which is known wisely, may be pursued ardently. And in this matter I give you this advice first, that, how great so ever love of pious continence you feel to be in you, you ascribe it to the favor of God, and give Him thanks, Who of His Holy Spirit hath freely given unto you so much, as that, His love being shed abroad in your heart, the love of a better good should take away from you the permission of a lawful matter. For it was His gift to you that you should

not wish to marry, when it was lawful, in order that now it should not be lawful, even if you wished; and that by this means the wish not to do it might be the more settled, lest what were now unlawful be done, which was not done even when lawful; and that, a widow of Christ, you should so far attain as to see your daughter also a virgin of Christ; for whilst you are praying as Anna, she hath become what Mary was. These by how much the more you know them to be gifts of God, by so much the more are you by the same gifts blessed; yea, rather, you are not so otherwise than as you know from Whom you have what you have. For listen to what the Apostle said on this matter, "But we have received not the spirit of this world, but the Spirit Which is of God, that we may know what things have been given to us by God." Forsooth many have many gifts of God, and by not knowing from Whom they have them, come to boast themselves with impious vanity. But there is no one blessed with the gifts of God, who is ungrateful to the Giver. Forasmuch as, also, whereas in the course of the sacred Mysteries we are bidden to "lift up our hearts," it is by His help that we are able, by Whose bidding we are admonished; and therefore it follows, that, of this so great good of the heart lifted up, we give not the glory to ourselves as of our own strength, but render thanks unto our Lord God. For of this we are straightway admonished, that "this is meet," "this is right." You remember whence these words are taken, you recognize by what sanction, and by how great holiness they are commended within. Therefore hold and have what you have received, and return thanks to the Giver. For, although it be yours to receive and have, yet you have that, which you have received; forasmuch as to one waxing proud, and impiously glorying of that which he had, as though he had it of himself, the Truth saith by the Apostle, "But what hast thou, which thou hast not received? But, if you have received, why do you boast, as if you had not received?"

21. These things I am compelled to admonish by reason of certain little discourses of some men, that are to be shunned and avoided, which have begun to steal through the ears unto the minds of many, being (as must be said with tears) hostile to the grace of Christ, which go to persuade that we count not as necessary for us prayer unto the Lord, that we enter not into temptation. For they so essay to defend the free will of man, as that by it alone, even without help of the grace of God, we are able to fulfill what is commanded us of God. And thus it follows, that the Lord in vain said, "Watch and pray, lest ye enter into temptation;" and in vain daily in the Lord's Prayer itself we say, "Lead us not into temptation." For if it is of our own power alone that we be not overcome by temptation, why do we pray that we enter not, nor be led into it? Rather let us do what is of our own free will, and most absolute power; and let us mock at the Apostle, saying, "God is faithful, Who will not suffer you to be tempted above what ye are able;" and let us oppose him, and say, Why seek I of the Lord, what He hath set in my own power? But far be it, that he be so minded, who is sound minded. Wherefore let us seek that He may give, what He bids us that we have. For to this end He bids us have this, which as yet we have not, to admonish as what to seek; and that when we shall have found the power to do what He hath bidden, we may understand, of this also, whence we have received it; lest, being puffed and lifted up by the spirit of this world, we know not what things

have been given unto us of God. Wherefore the free choice of the human will we by no means destroy, when the Grace of God, by which the free choice itself is helped, we deny not with ungrateful pride, but rather set forth with grateful piety. For it is ours to will: but the will itself is both admonished that it may arise, and healed, that it may have power; and enlarged, that it may receive; and filled, that it may have. For were not we to will, certainly neither should we receive the things that are given, nor should we have. For who would have continence, (among the rest of the gifts of God to speak of this rather, of which I am speaking to you,) who, I say, would have continence, unless willing? forasmuch as also no one would receive unless willing. But if you ask, Whose gift it is, that it can be by our will received and had? listen to Scripture; yea, rather, because thou knows, recollect what thou hast read, "Whereas I knew," saith he, "that no one can be continent, unless God give it, and this itself was of wisdom, to know whose gift it was. "Great are these two gifts, wisdom and continence; wisdom, forsooth, whereby we are formed in the knowledge of God; but continence, whereby we are not conformed unto this world. But God bids us that we be both wise and continent, without which goods we cannot be just and perfect. But let us pray that He give what He bids, by helping and inspiring, Who hath admonished us what to will by commanding and calling. Whatsoever of this He hath given, let us pray that He preserve; but what He hath not given as yet, let us pray that He supply; yet let us pray and give thanks for what we have received; and for what we have not yet received, from the very fact that we are not ungrateful for what we have received, let us trust that we shall receive it. For He, Who hath given power unto the faithful who are married to contain from adulteries and fornications, Himself hath given unto holy virgins and widows to contain from all sexual intercourse; in the case of which virtue now the term inviolate chastity or continence is properly used. Or is it haply that from Him indeed we have received continence, but from ourselves have wisdom? What then is it that the Apostle James saith, "But if any of you lack wisdom, let him ask of God, Who giveth unto all liberally, and upbraided not, and it shall be given unto him." But on this question, already in other little works of ours, so far as the Lord hath helped us, we have said many things; and at other times, so far as through Him we shall be able, when opportunity is given, we will speak.

22. Now it has been my wish on this account to say something on this subject, by reason of certain of our brethren most friendly and dear to us, and without willful guilt indeed entangled in this error, but yet entangled; who think, that, when they exhort any to righteousness and piety, their exhortation will not have force, unless the whole of that, wherein they would work upon man that man should work, they set in the power of man, not helped by the grace of God, but put forth by the alone choice of the free will; as though there can be free will to perform a good work, unless set free by the gift of God! And they mark not that this very thing themselves also have by the gift of God, that with such power they exhort, as to excite the dull wills of men to enter upon a good life, to enkindle the cold, to correct such as are in error, to convert such as are turned aside, to pacify such as are opposed. For thus they are able to succeed in persuading what they would persuade to, or if they work not these

things in the wills of men, what is their work? wherefore speak they? Let them leave them rather to their own choice. But if in them they work these things, what? I pray, doth man, in the will of man, work so great things by speaking, and doth God work nothing there by helping? Yea rather, with how great so ever power of discourse man may prevail, as that by skill of discussion, and sweetness of speech, he in the will of man implant truth, nourish charity, by teaching remove error, by exhortation remove sloth, "Neither he who planted is anything, nor he who watered, but God Who giveth the increase." For in vain would the workman use all means without, unless the Creator should work secretly within. I hope therefore that this letter of mine by the worthy deed of your Excellence will soon come into the hands of such also; on this account I thought that I ought to say something on this subject. Next that both you yourself, and whatsoever other widows shall read this, or hear it read, may know that you make more advance unto the love and profession of the good of continence by your own prayers than by our exhortations; forasmuch as if it be any help to you that our addresses also are supplied to you, the whole must be assigned to His grace, "in Whose Hand," as it is written, "are both we and our discourses."

23. If, therefore, you had not as yet vowed unto God widowed continence, we would assuredly exhort you to vow it; but, in that you have already vowed it, we exhort you to persevere. And yet I see that I must so speak as to lead those also who had as yet thought of marriage to love it and to seize on it. Therefore let us give ear unto the Apostle, "She who is unmarried," saith he, "is careful about the things of the Lord, to be holy both in

body and spirit; but she who is married is careful about the things of the world, how to please her husband." He saith not, is careful about the things of the world, so as not to be holy; but certainly that that marriage holiness is less, in regard of that portion of cares, which hath thought of the pleasure of the world. Whatever, therefore, I of earnest purpose of mind would be expended also on these things whereby she would have to please a husband, the unmarried Christian woman ought in a certain way to gather and bring together unto that earnest purpose whereby she is to please the Lord. And consider, Whom she pleases, who pleases the Lord; and assuredly she is by so much the more blessed by how much the more she pleases Him; but by how much the more her thoughts are of the things of the world, by so much the less does she please Him. Therefore do ye with all earnest purpose please Him, Who is "'fair of form above the sons of men." For that ye please Him, it is by His grace which is "shed abroad on His lips." Please ye Him in that portion of thought also, which would be occupied by the world, in order to please a husband. Please ye Him, Who displeased the world, in order that such as please Him might be set free from the world. For This One, fair of form above the sons of men, men saw on the Cross of the Passion; "and He had not form or beauty, but His face cast down, and His posture unseemly." Yet from this unseemliness of your Redeemer flowed the price of your beauty, but of a beauty within, for "all the beauty of the King's daughter is within." By this beauty please ye Him, this beauty order ye with studious care and anxious thought. He loves not dyes of deceits; the Truth delighted in things that are true, and He, if you recognize what you have read, is called the Truth. "I am," saith He, "the Way, and the Truth, and the

Life." Run ye to Him through Him, please ye Him of Him; live ye with Him, in Him, of Him. With true affections and holiest chastity love ye to be loved by such a Husband.

24. Let the inner ear of the virgin also, thy holy child, hear these things. I shall see how far she goes before you in the Kingdom of That King: it is another question. Yet ye have found, mother and daughter, Him, Whom by beauty of chastity ye ought to please together, having despised, she all, you second, marriage. Certainly if there were husbands whom ye had to please, by this time, perhaps, you would feel ashamed to adorn yourself together with your daughter; now let it not shame you, to set yourselves to do what may adorn you both together; because it is not matter of blame, but of glory, that ye be loved both together by That One. But white and red, feigned and laid on with paints, ye would not use, even if ye had husbands; not thinking that they were fit persons for you to deceive, or yourselves such as ought to deceive; now therefore That King, Who had longed for the beauty of His Only Spouse, of Whom ye are members, do ye with all truth together please, together cleave unto; she with virginal chastity, you with widowed continence, both with spiritual beauty. In which beauty also her grandmother, and your mother-in-law, who by this time surely hath grown old, is beautiful together with you. Forsooth whilst charity carries the vigor of this beauty into things that are before, length of years caused not in it a wrinkle. You have with you a holy aged woman, both in your house and in Christ, whom to consult concerning perseverance; how you are to fight with this or that temptation, what you are to do, that it may be the more

easily overcome; what safeguard you are to take, that it may not easily again lay wait; and if there be any thing of this sort, she teaches you, who is now by time fixed, by love a well-wisher, by natural affection full of cares, by age secure. Do you specially, do you in such things consult her, who hath made trial of what you have made trial of. For your child sings that song, which in the Apocalypse none save virgins can sing. But for both of you she prays more carefully than for herself, but she is fuller of care for her granddaughter, for whom there remains a longer space of years to overcome temptations; but you she sees nearer to her own age, and mother of a daughter of such an age, as that, had you seen her married, (which now is not lawful, and far be it from her,) I think you would have blushed to bear children together with her. How much then is it that now remains to you of a dangerous age, who are on this account not called a grandmother, in order that together with your daughter you may be fruitful in offspring of holy thoughts and works? Therefore, not without reason is the grandmother fuller of care for her, for whom you also the mother; because both what she hath vowed is greater, and the whole of what she hath just now begun remains to her. May the Lord hear her prayers, that ye may holily follow her good deserts, Who in youth gave birth to the flesh of your husband, in old age travailed with the heart of your daughter. Therefore do ye all, alike and with one accord, by conduct please, by prayers press upon, That One Husband of One Wife, in Whose Body by One Spirit ye are living.

25. The past day returns not hereafter, and after yesterday proceeds to-day, and after to-day will proceed

to-morrow; and, lo, all times and the things of time pass away, that there may come the promise that shall abide; and "whoso shall have persevered even unto the end, this one shall be saved." If the world is now perishing, the married woman, for whom bear she? Or in heart about to bear, and in flesh not about to bear, why doth she marry? But if the world is still about to last, why is not He more loved, by Whom the world was made? If already enticements of this life are failing, there is not anything for a Christian soul with desire to seek after; but if they shall yet remain, there is what with holiness he may despise. For the one of these two there is no hope of lust, in the other greater glory of charity. How many or how long are the very years, in which the flower of carnal age seems to flourish? Some females having thoughts of marriage, and with ardor wishing it, whilst they are being despised or put off, on a sudden have grown old, so as that now they would feel shame, rather than desire, to marry. But many having married, their husbands having set out into distant countries very soon after their union, have grown aged expecting their return, and, as though soon left widows, at times have not even attained so as at least as old women to receive their old men on their return. If therefore, when betrothed bridegrooms despised or delayed, or when husbands were abroad, carnal desire could be restrained from commission of fornication or adultery, why cannot it be restrained from commission of sacrilege? If it hath been repressed, when being deferred it was glowing, why is it not put down, when having been cut off it had grown cold? For they in greater measure endure glowing of desire, who despair not of the pleasure of the same desire. But whoso of unmarried persons vow chastity to God, withdraw that very hope, which is the fuel of love. Hence with more ease is desire bridled, which is kindled by no expectation; and yet, unless against this prayer be made, in order to overcome it, itself as unlawful is the more ardently wished for.

26. Therefore let spiritual delights succeed to the place of carnal delights in holy chastity; reading, prayer, psalm, good thought, frequency in good works, hope of the world to come, and a heart upward; and for all these giving of thanks unto the Father of lights, from Whom, without any doubt, every good gift, and every perfect gift, as Scripture bears witness, cometh down. For when, instead of the delights of married women, which they have in the flesh of their husbands, the use of other carnal delights is taken, as it were to solace them, why should I speak of the evils which follow, when the Apostle hath said in short, that the widow, who lives in delights, living is dead. But far be it from you, that ye be taken with lust of riches instead of lust of marriage, or that in your hearts money succeed to the place of love of a husband. For looking into men's conversation, we have often found by experience, that in certain persons, when wantonness hath been restrained, avarice hath increased. For, as, in the senses themselves of the body, they who see not hear more keenly, and discern many things by touch, nor have such as have the use of their eyes so great life in their touch; and in this instance it is understood that, when the exertion of the power of attention hath been restrained in one approach, that is, of the eyes, it puts itself forth into other senses, more ready with keenness to distinguish, as though it essayed to supply from the one what was denied in the other; thus also often carnal lust, being restrained from pleasure of sensual intercourse, with greater strength

reaches itself forth to desire money, and when turned away from the one, turns itself with more glow of passion to the other. But in you let the love of riches grow cold together with the love of marriage, and let a pious use of what property you possess be directed to spiritual delights, that your liberality wax warm rather in helping such as are in want than in enriching covetous persons. Forsooth into the heavenly treasury are sent not gifts to the covetous, but alms to the needy, which above measure help the prayers of widows. Fastings, also, and watchings, so far as they disturb not health, if they be spent in praying, singing psalms, reading, and meditating in the Law of God, even the very things which seem laborious are turned into spiritual delights. For no way burdensome are the labors of such as love, but even of themselves delight, as of such as hunt, fowl, fish, gather grapes, traffic, delight themselves with some game. It matters therefore what beloved. For, in the case of what is loved, either there is no labor, or the labor also is loved. And consider how it should be matter for shame and grief, if there be pleasure in labor, to take a wild beast, to fill cask and purse, to cast a ball, and there be no pleasure in labors to win God!

27. Indeed in all spiritual delights, which unmarried women enjoy, their holy conversation ought also to be with caution; lest haply, though their life be not evil through haughtiness, their report be evil through negligence. Nor are they to be listened to, whether they be holy men or women, when (upon occasion of their neglect in some matter being blamed, through which it comes to pass that they fall into evil suspicion, from which they know that their life is far removed) they say that it is

enough for them their conscience before God, despising what men think of them, not only imprudently but also cruelly; when they slay the souls of others; whether of such as blaspheme the way of God, who following their suspicion are displeased at what is the chaste life of the Saints, as though it were shameful, or of such also as make excuse, and imitate, not what they see, but what they think. Wherefore whosoever guards his life from charges of shameful and evil deeds, does good to himself; but whosoever guards his character too, is merciful also towards others. For unto ourselves our own life is necessary, unto others our character; and certainly even what we mercifully minister unto others, for their health, abounds also to our own profit. Whence not in vain the Apostle, "We provide good things," saith he, "not only before God, but also before men;" also he saith, "Please ye all men through all things; even as I also please all men through all things, not seeking what is of profit unto myself, but what unto many, that they may be saved." Also in a certain exhortation he says, "For the rest, brethren, whatsoever things are true, whatsoever things are holy, whatsoever things are just, whatsoever things are pure, whatsoever things are most dear, whatsoever things are of good report; if any virtue, if any praise, these things think on, which ye have both learned, and received, and heard, and seen in me." You see how among many things, unto which by exhortation he admonished them, he neglected not to set, "whatsoever things are of good report;" and in two words included all things, where he saith, "if any virtue, if any praise." For unto virtue pertain the good things of which He made mention above; but good report unto praise. I think that the Apostle took not the praise of men for any great thing, saying in another place, "But to me it is the least thing, that I be judged of you, or of day of man;" and in another place, "If I were pleasing men, I should not be a servant of Christ;" and again, "For our glory is this, the testimony of our conscience." But of these two, that is, of a good life, and a good report, or as is said more shortly, of virtue and praise, the one for his own sake he most wisely kept, the other for the sake of others he most mercifully provided. But, forasmuch as human caution, how great so ever, cannot on every side avoid most malevolent suspicions, when for our good report we shall have done whatever we rightly can, if any, either by falsely pretending evil things of us, or from believing evil of us, endeavor to stain our fair fame, let there be present the solace of conscience, and clearly also the joy, in that our reward is great in Heaven, even when men say many evil things of us, and we yet live godly and righteously. For that reward is as the pay of such as serve as soldiers, through the arms of righteousness, not only on the right hand, but on the left also; that is to say, through glory and mean estate, through ill report and good report.

28. Go on therefore in your course, and run with perseverance, in order that ye may obtain; and by pattern of life, and discourse of exhortation, carry away with you into this same your course, whomsoever ye shall have had power. Let there not bend you from this earnest purpose, whereby ye excite many to follow, the complaint of vain persons, who say, How shall the human race subsist, if all shall have been continent? As though it were for any other reason that this world is delayed, save that the predestined number of the Saints be fulfilled, and were this the sooner fulfilled, assuredly the end of the world would not be put

off. Nor let it stay you from your earnest purpose of persuading others to the same good ye have, if it be said to you, Whereas marriage also is good, how shall there be all goods in the Body of Christ, both the greater, forsooth, and the lesser, if all through praise and love of continence imitate? In the first place, because with the endeavor that all be continent, there will still be but few, for "not all receive this word." But forasmuch as it is written, "Whoso can receive, let him receive;" then do they receive who can, when silence is not kept even toward those who cannot. Next, neither ought we to fear lest haply all receive it, and someone of lesser goods, that is, married life, be wanting in the body of Christ. For if all shall have heard, and all shall have received, we ought to understand that this very thing was predestinated, that married goods already suffice in the number of those members which so many have passed out of this life. For neither now, if all shall have been continent, will they give the honor of the continent to those who have already borne into the garners of the Lord the fruit thirty-fold, if that be understood of married good. Therefore all these goods will have there their place, although from this time no woman wish to be married, no man wish to marry a wife. Therefore without anxiety urge on whom ye can, to become what ye are; and pray with watchfulness and fervor, that by the help of the Right Hand of the Most High, and by the abundance of the most merciful grace of the Lord, ye may both persevere in that which ye are, and may make advances unto that which ye shall be.

29. Next I entreat you, by Him, from Whom ye have both received this gift, and hope for the rewards of this gift, that ye be mindful to set me also in your prayers

with all your household Church. Forsooth it hath come to pass in most proper order, that I should write unto your Mother now aged a letter concerning prayer; unto her, forsooth, it chiefly pertains by praying to contend on your behalf, who is less full of care for herself than for you; and that for you rather than for her I should compose this little work concerning widowed continence; because unto you it remained to overcome, what her age hath already overcome. But the holy virgin your child, if she desire aught concerning her profession from our labors, she hath a large book on Holy Virginity to read. Concerning the reading of which I had also admonished you, forasmuch as it contains many things necessary unto either chastity, that is, virginal and widowed, which things on this account I have here partly touched on lightly, partly altogether passed over, because I there discussed them more fully. May you persevere in the grace of Christ.

www.ingramcontent.com/pod-product-compliance
Lightning Source LLC
Chambersburg PA
CBHW052044070526
44584CB00018B/2611